PAGE TURNER

Valerie Macon

Acknowledgments:

Grateful Acknowledgement is made to the editors of the following publications in which the poems noted first appeared, some in different forms:

CCCC Red Clay Review 2021: Lady Left Out

CCCC Red Clay Review 2021: Sun, A Hard Task Master

Voice & Vision 2019: The Swans at Argyle Lake

Fly With Me 2017: How to Receive Abundance

INDEX

Dedication

For Mikel
Who Leaves No Page Unturned

Prologue

My friend approaches life
like she does her Book Club novel:
refuses to read the jacket,
would rather not know what's coming,
prefers to let the story surprise.
She says,

Who knows? Today your grits may be smooth,
the next day, full of lumps.

Life's a real Page Turner.

Smooth

Morning Rider

Tires hum, gears snap click,
bright breeze washes face.
Time cannot hold,
I pedal beyond its reach
where sun sneaks up on seams
of early lettuce still tucked in mist,
soybeans line up for morning muster,
a dog wakes from his dream, barks,
road slices fields of burst cotton,
rolls over hills where cows wade
in waves of dewy grass
and the sky has dropped its blue in ponds.

I'm as free as the crow flying over,
its caw echoing cross silent fields.

How to Receive Abundance

Crouch among bush beans,
knees pressed in warm soil.
Weave fingers through
jade leaf that shades
pods thick as pencils.
Pinch them from their stems,
smell earth and summer rain
as they thump the bucket.

Rake your spading fork
under the potato plant
after its yellow flower fades
and its leaf withers.
Cleave it from the earth,
tubers clinging to roots.
Rummage the soil, find
a buried golden spud, *Yeehaw!*
Then another, and another.   Howl

till neighbors pause their coffee cups,
turn their heads from cable news and wonder,
why such jubilation?

The Gardener Earns a Living

Through the kitchen window
I hear the gardener crooning,
skipping like a scratched record
over and over the same line.
He has been on his knees
for an hour, hunched over
blue rug juniper at the edge
of the neighbor's drive
plucking weeds, clipping overgrowth,
mopping his brow on his sleeve.

He throws in the music for free.

Sandra Plays the Piano

fingers brushing the keys,
sweeping silence aside.

Sunlight sifts through windows,
gilds dust.

Her shadow slants across the Grand,
slips up the wall.

Paper-white curtains rise and fall,
angel wings.

Bird Lesson

An early bird sits in a long leaf pine,
his pear-shape traced
in diamonds of early light.

Now is the time to hustle, to gather grub
before sun brightens and blisters the earth.
Yet he sits longer than any bird should,

king of the tree, easing into
this new day, his bird eyes sliding
over the fresh landscape of his domain.

Be Brave

I'm afraid of alligators, scared they will chase and eat me,
terrified of rattlesnakes that lunge, inject toxic venom,
and of sharks that rip while you ride a wave.

I'm afraid of small things: tics bearing Lyme disease,
brown recluse spiders with flesh-rotting bite,
red ants whose ambush burns and blisters.

But this morning I see a mirrored lake
alive with joyful ripples of fish,
birds flying over ecstatic with song, and I wonder:

do fish live in fear of a great blue heron,
do squirrels dread the snap and snatch of an eagle,
do mice worry they'll become snake snack?

Every animal is someone's meal.
Yet they live their lives in exuberant expectancy
of the day at hand: singing, croaking , chirping,
hissing, cawing and boldly attending to the tasks of life
until it is no more.

Paw Boost Alerts

Posted on Neighbor Blog:
Today at 3 pm Zeus went missing
in red collar, black walking harness.

Ben in Cottonwood writes
he'll keep an eye out, advises
blasting it on Paw Boost.

Gus, the orange-and-cream cat,
blue-collared and friendly but scared,
slips away while his owner
sweeps the garage.

Choco, one-blue-one-brown-eyed pup,
leaps his fence under cover of night,
is spotted camping on Sunset Lake Road,
but vanishes before sunrise.

Mr. Teddy Bear, tabby cat, fled collarless
last night, unlike him his owner says,
although he's sure Teddy is out honing
his hunting skills.

Eleven pm, Zeus is found outside his fence
still dragging his leash.

Living Fearless

Just ahead, a man in a black Camaro
hangs his muscle-cut arm out the window.
His hand taps a breezy beat on the door.

. . . .

Keep your arms and hands inside
the car or you could lose them
my father often said, warning
of a girl who lost her limb this way.

On a stopped school bus one day,
I reached out the window, grabbed a branch.
As the bus pulled away, an angry rustle
of leaves severed from the limb.

Consequences were swift—
the bus jarred to a halt; scowling,
the driver staggered towards me,
scribbled the dreaded after-school-suspension slip.

. . . .

Fearless, I roll down my window,
hang my arm out, tap along
with the man in the black Camaro.

Birds' Point of View

This morning
there's twitter in the rafters
of Terminal A.
Bird heads swivel
left then right
watching humans
try to fly.

Humans
start before daylight,
hustle to park, wrestle
bags onto shuttles, stand
in twisted lines, gasp
to their gate
then stuff their tails
into tiny seats
for ten-hour flights.
For amusement, they buy
inflight movies.

Birds titter because
their flight is smooth!
They open their eyes,
fluff their feathers,
snatch grub from the earth,
take flight.
And for laughs, sit on a wire
and watch humans.
Free.

Looking Down

The poetry of the earth is never dead. John Keats

As the plane ascends, terrain spreads map-like,
shadow floats on water,
boats slash its surface.

Pools of land appear. Cars crawl,
silverfish on road ribbons,
houses in board-game clusters.

An island looms, helmet shaped,
waves trace its shore in white foam.

The plane banks, sky and sea smear
into tilted line; when it levels,
only glowing gold ocean.

In the Language of Trees

The root work comes first:
burrow, elongate, expand;
then spring stalk that lengthens
and widens into trunk
crowned with leafed branches.
Iron core, straight as a spear, noble.
In the language of trees, shape speaks.

Often, one growing upright
bends around another, or bows
and warps horizontal, or bears
knots and scars of a strike,
or a strangle of vines.
Some are lopped at a power line, but
growth is unstoppable.

Gifts of the Sea

At the beach the broken gets sifted.
Ocean wash scatters pieces,
rolls the shards out to sea.

A storm can pile perfect shells on shore.
If you don't mind dirty hands,
you might find a Scotch Bonnet
among the soggy piles of seaweed.

Pay attention to the tides.
When waves roll in low and frothy
they gift whole sand dollars, starfish,
augers and olive shells among the shuck.

Rarely will you leave the beach empty-handed.

Lunching with JoJo

at Ella's of Calabash, she slides away
her Deluxe Seafood Platter,
centers her side of quivering oysters
glistening on a bed of Iceberg lettuce.

Fish fork poised, she frames strategy,
then teases out the gray meat, transfers it
to Triscuit, tucks it into a slick lump.
Neat. It oozes off the cracker.
Frowning, she nudges it back to center.

She dollops horseradish, splashes Texas Pete,
sluices fresh lemon, then sends it slipping
down her throat—one,
                                        then another,
                                                    then another . .

Feast in Famine

From a far flung cubical in a gray maze
where backs bend over task,
eyes strain on screens, a foreign sound
rises above phone chatter.

Not the humdrum lunch noise of
plastic bag crinkle, the cardboard rip
of a Lean Cuisine box, or the snap-whoosh
startle of an opened can drink.

But a curious clink of silver on china,
musical clash of fork against knife,
pop of cork and glug of wine
pouring into a fine crystal goblet.

The sound, a feast of sweet tones
for desk jockeys chewing on mundane work.

The Swans at Argyle Lake

their necks half hearts,
glide, trail rings of ripples
like bridal veils.

The sun is high noon,
a hazy smolder,
the pond, a slow simmer.

A child skips and giggles,
pitches a crust of bread
into the steamy soup.

Necks snap to exclamation points.
Red bills trace the tiny favor
through its bleached-sky arc.

Clatter of beating wings,
tangle of necks,
snow of feathers,

greedy snatch.

Flamingo

He faces into the wind
and like the origami crane
creases one leg
folds it into his belly feathers
stands plumb on the other
in pure pink
like a graceful vase
set on a pedestal
then pivots his neck
and buries his head
in the salmon fluff of his back.

Contender

A toddler, blond hair snatched
in a bow, curls around
her mother's pregnant belly.
Mom clips the girl's tiny nails
then adorns each digit
with a dot of polish.
Princess fans her fingers, smiles
at the sparkle of pink.
Mom then lifts the girl's legs
onto the mound of her belly
and pampers the toes,
trimming and painting
while the child lounges content
in this mother-lode of care
before Sister Princess arrives.

At the Spring Outdoor Concert

Harriet, taken by a tune,
cannot stay in her seat.
Shoulders rocking, she coaxes
Don to the dance floor,
fingers popping over her head,
hips bumping this way and that.

Don, a minimalist,
pulses one knee to the beat,
watches her strut circles around him
like a prairie chicken.

A sliver of moon
smiles on the couple.

The Transcend Water Show

City Creek Center
Salt Lake City, Utah

The fountain reels
an Irish step dance,
spouts, circles and spins
tornados, thunders into rain,
fire jigs with water,
whirls, mingles, pauses mid-air,
dips, jets, umbrellas,
tumbles in sequenced showers,
erupts a riot of flame and water,
launches, rockets, aborts,
beats like the loud, crisp clap
of a hard jig shoe,
slap tap, slap tap, slap tap.

Lumpy

Garden Run Amuck

Chaos started with house-hugging evergreens
in tidy loaves, a bed of red zinnias,
a stand of blue-eyed daisies,
a gleaming gazing ball.

Vines made a slow creep to a tangle of bush
and scattered yard menagerie—wind spinners,
gnomes, toads bearing lanterns,
kissing Dutch figures, whirligig flamingos.

The whine of lawn widgets scared the birds
so they flew far from the snarl of juniper
and top-heavy crepe myrtle hiding
a host of feeders lost in the jumble.

Battling Aliens

Every night aliens come
dropping their eggs over front lawns.
In the morning their spawn hatches
mushrooms of all forms:
toad stools, parasols, puffballs,
stinkhorns, shaggy manes, and
a host of swollen buttons.
They pop in fairy rings.
Touch them, if you dare.

Some are fleshy, others soft,
spongy, hollow, crumbly.
One, stalkless, lumpy as a toad,
hard and dug-in like field rock,
needs a boot to dislodge it.
Another nurses on the earth,
and when pulled away, spits a gush of milk.
One with a tough shank lets out
a startled squeak when yanked.

Black Rat Snake

He shelters in my crawlspace,
loops around the water heater,
then slips out of his skin
leaving it like empty sausage casing.
I spot him scaling the foundation wall
standing straight up.
He appears coiled in a tangle of chicory,
and later, stretched out basking
on a bed of yard leaves
until Rascal's high-pitched howl
sends him winding.

One day, stalking supper
of frog or lizard or mouse,
heedless of hazard, he slinks
into Alice's yard where
hiding in shadows, hoe raised,
she separates his head.

In the Lion's Den

At the playground my grandson toddles
see-saw to swing to spinner. I hover,
hoisting him onto rocking ducks,
spotting him up ladders, off slides.

A boy follows us, hangs
upside-down from monkey bars, tells me:

My name is Daniel, that's D-A-N-I-E-L.

He flips into a one-arm dangle.

*I was named after a guy in the Bible
called Daniel. He was thrown into
a lion's den but didn't get eaten.*

He slips down a twisted slide.

*I don't know my mama
or my daddy's name.
So don't ask.*

I ponder, don't ask.

Watch me! Daniel shouts
as he spins my grandson dizzy
on the Merry Go Round
in this lions den,

where no one else is watching.

Father-Son Breakfast

The father's t-shirt reads
Time Spent Fishing is Never Wasted,
his blond hair spiked, muscles pumped.

The boy chatters about
        his dog Lego . . .
                his teacher Miss Tickle . . .
                        his friend Charlie. . . .
all the while hoping Dad
will look up from his iPhone,
cast a glance at him.

Hanging out at Bam Bam's Cafe during Flight Delay

I've taken the last seat,
across from them—
he, barely out of braces:
"I was *like* so stoked". . .
"I was *like,* really dude?". . .
she, just into bras,
her liquid blue eyes full of worship.
I try not to listen to their words
that bubble over the murmur of
café chatter and flight announcements.

Suddenly they kiss with the passion of
Spider Man and Mary Jane.
Trapped in their moment,
I turn tomato faced, try to shift
focus to my fork slicing a wedge
of omelet, watch it ooze cheese.
I gaze into the foam of my
chai latte, until at last, heaving
backpacks over their shoulders,
they head off into the rumble
of airport crowd.

At the Movies

the line stalls
as the ticket taker tries again
to scan the e-ticket
on an iPhone cellophaned in cling wrap.

The owner, a teen in sullied clothing,
weedy hair, horn rimmed specs,
defends his plastic hack:
it keeps the phone clean—protected.

He resists unwrapping it.
His date, also rumpled,
chimes her support:
an extra shield against soil.

But, in the end, the phone must be peeled.
Afterwards, the couple stands buffing
its screen and case with tattered shirttails, then
rewrapping it, prophylactic in tidy plastic.

There It Is

Eyes rolling
palms rotating
either side of her head
she asks me
did you ever have an ear worm?

says—

it crawled in
while washin dishes with my brother
him dancin
whirlin his dish rag
singin like a fool

If you wanna get down
I'm gonna show you the way,
whoomp! There it is!

worm bored into my head
been stuck loopin round in there
days now

out of control.   She sings—

Let me hear you say
Whoomp chaka laka chaka laka
Whoomp! There it is!

I start singing along.
The earworm wiggles
out her ear
crawls into mine.

Wash Me White as Snow

The air is heat and soap and lint.
Tumbling clothes murmur in drums.
The attendant mumbles
on her cell phone over monotonous
low-level drone of football commentary.

He's been long at the laundry
working down high-piled hampers.
Clothes sloshing and spinning in Speed Queens.
Heaving knots of wet wash into dryers.
Feeding fistfuls of quarters into slots.

Now he waits on a steel folding chair,
head bowed, hands clasped,
lips moving as in unvoiced prayer . . .

Disquiet in Church

Clean-scrubbed, dressed
in Sunday's frilly best,
two sisters, four and six,
perch on pew beside grandma.

Soon the smaller, sly girl presses
her ear onto big sister's arm.
Big sister, angelic, slides away.
The tormentor follows,
continues to vex, ear on arm.
Grandma's ominous eye
ends the nonsense.

The small vixen slants
her sister a look,
more to come. . .

Vultures

A kettle of black vultures glides,
wings spread wide, tracking
plumes of odor. They wheel
and soar in tightening circles
then descend over road kill,
and with stunning efficiency,
a committee strips the carrion clean.

.   .   .   .   .   .

After church dinner, the Cleanup Committee,
four black-aproned women,
flock around the turkey carcass
and claw scraps of flesh off the bones
for tomorrow's kettle of soup.
In two minutes they've picked it
down to a scrubbed skeleton.

Snowball Shack

A line snakes behind
while I cull the hundred
exotic choices: Gummy Shark,
Pucker Patch, Toothpaste . . .
I sweat, decision disabled,
then blurt

Vanilla

I sit on a sun-drenched bench, lick
my boring white cone, vexed
I did not pick Tiger's Blood,
Fireball, Fuzzy Monkey,
Maui Wowee, Dill Pickle,
Pink Lady Cream.

Tomorrow—Wild Thang

Waitress Tech Woes

Greet guests within one minute. Check.
Be welcoming, cheerful. Check.
Make eye contact, give your name. Check.
But now, Betty is having tech trouble.

She hovers over the iPad menu,
hunting hard-to-find items,
her temples pearled with sweat.

She favors the heft of paper pad,
sharp pencil behind the ear,
a holler to the kitchen.

Finally, she pokes in her order: grits,
flapjacks, whipped butter, warm syrup.
Sends it soaring through cloud to cook.

Fast Food

The line at Mario's Pizza twists out the door.
Counter clerk hollers to pie slingers:
Sauce 'em all, cheese 'em all.
Slingers bellow: *Swingin' hot!*

Man wearing a "Beer is My Friend" tee
calls out to busy back crew, *Hey Betty!*
He waves a hand thick as a pork chop, then orders.
Counter girl yells: *Fly pie!*

Two women lean in, place their order,
Clerk barks: *Two Crazies!*
Bald guy in holey jeans orders.
Clerk calls: *Two peps!*

I order wings.
Flavor? her fingers ready over register.
I ask, *what do you have?*

She rotes through a fixed grin:
*Mild Hot BBQ Spicy BBQ Oven Roasted
Garlic Parmesan Bacon Honey Mustard
Lemon Pepper Teriyaki*

I ask, *Could you repeat that?*

Inventory on a Mountain Road

Ahead, a sign reads, *Antiques & Tomatoes*.
Around the bend, *Furniture & Lawnmowers*.
At the red light, *Dance & Oil Change*.
Down the hill, *Gold & Silver Coins & Fresh Eggs*.

I puzzle over this split stock:
heirlooms and fruit,
home decor and yard machinery,
boogie and auto maintenance,
precious metals and ova.

Peckish, I pull into a place that touts
Barbeque and Car Rentals,
order a sandwich and a hot cup of coffee.
I'm told no one orders coffee,
so they don't serve it.

For the Love of Selfies
(Iceland Vacation)

A teen teeters on mud-slicked outcrop
behind the waterfall at Seljalandsfoss,
his arms spread like Christ the Redeemer,
blowback lashing his garments.
In the backdrop, the fall thunders,
froths over cliffs, crashes into pools.
He extends a selfie stick—

Another snapper scales the towering
basalt column cliffs at Reynisfjara,
balances on a tiny hexagon pinnacle,
fixes a grin—

At Black Sand Beach, a poser
stands on the brim beside a sign that reads:
Danger, Rogue Waves, Stay Away from Shore.
White foam roils behind him, he pastes a smile.

A wall of water rolls in—snaps him up.

Another Day on the Big W Casino Boat

Fruit machines blaze
with promise of payouts,
bonus rounds, multipliers,
enticing gamblers to dig deeper.

The bemused push coins
into Triple Twister, The Big Bopper,
Betty Boop's Love Meter,
pumping the long arm
with the rhythm of an oil rig
drilling for liquid gold.

Later, wells dried up.
Rows of one-arm bandits stand idle,
their hoppers overflowing.
The fleeced slouch against walls,
pockets inside out.

A rumpled woman slumps on a chair
working her toothless gums.

Blemish

She paces her duties: massaging feet,
wrapping legs in hot towels, painting toes,
unmindful, it seems, of the eggplant bruise
that welts her face brow to chin,
or that her wound unsettles me.

I ache to ask, *whose banana-bunch fist
has thwacked you?* I want to shake her
from her nightmare's grip,
to speak comforting words,
take her hand, walk her out.

I'm struck by turn of thought:
Was this woman born slapped?
Have the years rendered her
resigned to bear this birth blemish
conscious of it no more?

She portions hot oils into salt scrub,
massages my feet, wraps my legs,
paints my toes "Purple With A Purpose".

Sun, a Hard Taskmaster

Early morning it points a finger
through the front door sidelight,
spreads shame throughout the house.

It shines on the smudged granite countertop,
spotlights leftovers on dark wood floor,
exposes a dust bunny hunkered in a corner,
reveals a powder haze on the glass TV stand,
accents fingerprints pressed on a framed print
and a web draped from vaulted ceiling.

But the sun is no respecter of persons.
Soon it creeps up the east side
of a neighbor's house and peeps in her windows.

What the Squatter Left

Among the rows of orange, green
and breezy blue homes that line
the cobbled streets of Old San Juan,
an abandoned house on Calle Luna
chills like a B-rated horror set.

Behind brackish windows
in empty rooms of peeling walls
and breath of damp and guano,
are the sacrifices of a squatter:

brush and twisted tube of paste on a seedy sink,
a soiled mattress, grounded,
scattered needles,

and sketched across mildewed wall, graffiti:
a naked woman, eyeballs on her boobs.

Graffiti Writer

Tagging is almost an addiction,
danger the drug: ducking police,
crawling under barbed wire . . .

Always look for places to get in and out.
Once tore up my bubble parka trying to
drag myself through a hole in a fence.

Keep a spray can handy to satisfy the itch.
Signs, bridges, tunnels—my canvas.
Edgy pieces in dangerous places—heaven.

Best place to work, the sidetracks: solitary,
dark, the eerie huff hiss of compressors;
an express blows by, flies garbage everywhere.

Sometimes get to paint a brand-new train,
still smells of fresh motor oil.
Haters say my work is vandalism.

But if you get away with it, it's art.

Remnants

The estate sale has been going on
for several days. Today,
everything's seventy-five percent off.

I never met them, whose house
is being picked over,
twenty years a passing wave
while they bent over yard work.
Today, curious neighbors and strangers
trek a weedy path to their door.

Inside, faded art prints, blank-eyed
dolls assembled on a couch, costume
jewelry laid out on a dingy bedspread,
clothes tangled on the closet floor,
a tricycle rusting in the yard.

The agent doesn't know
what happened to them.
Tomorrow morning he'll call Goodwill
to haul off what's left.

Grand Finales

I.
The Zumba instructor gushed
a nosebleed during class,
soaking clumps of coarse
paper towel pressed to his nose.
Nurses Zumba'd to seat him,
tilt his head, pinch his nostrils,
while he continued to salsa.
He said he just wanted to finish.

II.
The hairdresser's heart attack came
while cutting my hair, yet he continued
to clip away. Clutching his chest,
said he just wanted to finish the cut.
I begged him to stop, gripped the armrests,
stiff with fear that I might be
his final loose end.
At the last snip, ambulance arrived.

Keeping up with Canes

Suddenly, granny realizes
she's no longer leaning on her cane.
After a frenzy, finds it hooked
on a dining room chair back.

Her walking sticks loiter under tables,
hang out on door handles,
creep under car seats.

At the grocery store,
she turns to select a cereal
and her favorite designer cane
goes missing from her shopping cart.

In the surgeon's waiting room
six weeks out from hip replacement,
she remembers leaving her quad
at Walmart's pharmacy counter.

She recalls they have a young employee
tasked with rounding up forsaken canes
from store aisles and parking lots
and shepherding them into Lost and Found.

But this time when she returns for it,
she finds it still standing in line.

Lady Left Out

Lady, Grandpa's brindle boxer
who smells like moldy bread,
is barricaded in the mudroom
just off the kitchen where people
chatter and laugh and sing
on a Sunday afternoon.

Her funk seeps into the kitchen,
mingles with the meatballs,
the sauce and cheese of the lazania.

All afternoon she yearns, poking
her snout through slats in her barricade.
Her paws click clack the speckled tiles.
She wines up a full-throated woof,
springs at the gate.

Down Lady! Grandpa scolds.
She collapses, a heap of defeat. Repeats.

Hours later, she is released.
Guests gone, her freedom an empty victory.

Today's Agenda

Staff has parked
a clutch of wheelchairs
in the nursing home hallway.
Three women
hang on their bones,
talk to each other
in a language of eyeballs:

You should have seen me in my heyday, one says.
I'm trapped in this broken body, says another.
Bingo! says the third.

Mission Accomplished

Scratched into rock near cliff's edge at
Cabo Rojo, Los Morrillos Lighthouse—

Casey Ginerich, Born Jan 21, 1987,
Fell Feb 11, 2011, Safely Home

Five young missionaries, first day of
service complete, trek a rugged foot path
up salt flats, zig zag sea grass and mangroves
to the pinnacle of Cabo Rojo's red cliffs
where Los Morrillos Light keeps watch
over churning Caribbean seas. This day,

Earth and Wind and Water conspire.
The Light stands spellbound
as a narrow ledge between two worlds
crumbles under your step, a gust
tumbles you over the edge, sea thunders
as it reaches up and folds you into its froth.

You raise your arms in surrender,
grasp the hands of God.

Sow, Harvest, Plow

There's a cycle to these fields:

soil tilled flat and ready
for rows of seeded hills,
green haze of new sprout,
acres heavy with harvest.

Stretches of earth plowed under.

The folks around here
sowed their soil in sweat,
grew crops of offspring,
harvested their rewards.

Many have been plowed under.

Epilogue

My friend listens to birds burble in branches,
swigs sweet tea from cut crystal chalices,
double scoops lemon cake into fine china cups
as she turns the pages,
always ready for that
next surprise.

CPSIA information can be obtained
at www.ICGtesting.com
Printed in the USA
LVHW082123110821
695091LV00011B/334